"STEELER PRIDE"

DOUG YENCHO

authorHOUSE®

AuthorHouse™
1663 Liberty Drive
Bloomington, IN 47403
www.authorhouse.com
Phone: 1-800-839-8640

First published by AuthorHouse   01/11/2012

ISBN: 978-1-4685-3901-1 (sc)
ISBN: 978-1-4685-3900-4 (hc)
ISBN: 978-1-4685-3899-1 (ebk)

Library of Congress Control Number: 2011963712

Printed in the United States of America

I am a fan of the game of football as well as a Steeler fan! Any and all information in this book is intended for fun and enjoyment purposes only and is in no way intended to offend any one person, or organization mentioned. It is intended in the spirit of competition and fan appreciation and is in no way affiliated with the NFL

Thank you and enjoy your reading with a sense of humor as it is intended.

Photo by **Kevin Archer**

A LITTLE LOOK BACK

The history of the Pittsburgh Steelers dates clear back to 1933 when they were known as the Pittsburgh Pirates. They used this name until 1940 when owner, Art Roonie, changed the name to the Steelers to represent the Steel town heritage of Pittsburgh. During the 1943 season, The name of the team was Changed again. Our Nation was at war. The Steelers could not come up with enough players to field a team. Neither could the Philadelphia Eagles so the two teams combined and were known as the Steagles. Again in 1944 the Steelers combined with another team. The Chicago Cardinals and were referred to unofficially as Car-Pitts or "The Carpets"

Now let me tell ya a little something about the Steelers back in those days. They sucked. I mean seriously. They had very few winning seasons and rarely made a post season appearance. They went through head coaches like I go through sox. They just couldn't seam to bring anything together until that fatefull day. The day a legend walked into Pittsburgh. January 27,1969. On this day, Chuck Noll was named head coach of the Pittsburgh Steelers.

Some major changes took place following the hiring of Chuck Noll. Along with the 1970 season came the AFL-NFL merger, The Steelers moved from the NFL Century division to the AFC Central, and they moved from Forbes Field to the brand new, Three Rivers Stadium. After selecting "Mean" Joe Greene as his first ever draft pick in 1969, he chose another man in 1970 who would soon become legendary in his own right. That man was Terry Bradshaw and to this day is one of only two NFL quarter backs to win 4 Super Bowl rings. Greene and Bradshaw were just 2 of the many legendary draft picks Chuck Noll would make over the next few years on his way to building a dynasty. Some say the team of the decade.

I say the Greatest team in the history of the game.

Over the next few years, the Steelers would show some major improvements from the early years. In 1972 they would win there first division title and host the first playoff game ever played in Three Rivers Stadium. That game was played against the Oakland Raiders and was won by Pittsburgh on the most famous play ever in football. The "Immaculate Reception". Pittsburgh would loose the next game to the once mighty, Miami Dolphins, but its all good. We were just getting started. Move over NFL. Here comes the most dominate force this game has ever seen!!

Chuck Noll would go on to lead the Steelers to an unprecedented four Super Bowl titles in a six year span. Winning championships in 1974,1975,1978,1979 It was remarkable to watch this to say the least. The best part of it all, we beat those bigmouthed, self proclaimed Americas Team, Dallas Crybaby's in two of these championships. But nothing can last forever huh? Are players aged. We were always winning so we weren't getting good draft picks and the team began to struggle again. They were still competitive but just could get back to the Super Bowl. So, after 23 seasons as the Head Coach of the Pittsburgh Steelers and a very impressive win loss record of 209 wins,156 losses and 1 tie, Chuck Noll retired after the 1991 season. He was, and still is, the only head coach ever to win four Super Bowls. Chuck . . . You were the man. Thank you for all you done!!!

And so a new era begins. Our new head coach. Bill Cowher. At the ripe old age of 34. He is, at this time, the youngest head coach in the game. Well. Lets see what he can do huh?

Cowher didn't do too bad. He took us to two more Super Bowls loosing in 1996 to the Cowboys and giving us our 5th Super Bowl ring in 2006. We consistently made the playoffs during the error of Cower Power. He resigned following the 2006 season. I don't know. He just didn't impress me as a coach. Just 1 Super Bowl win in 15 years? He had good teams to work with. Lots of talented players. Seams to me he shoulda won more. Oh well. He did one thing right. He brought us Ben Roethlisberger!!! . . . Ok two things. Cant forget Jarome Bettis!!!

Here comes Mike Tomlin. Now this guy I like. Two years as head coach. Two division titles. And yes, are 6th Super Bowl ring in his second year. The only team with 6 is who?. The Steelers . . . That's who! Oh yea. This is gonna get fun with this guy leading us. So sit back and enjoy the ride as I take you through the 2010 season with a game by game overview as well as a few stories a wanna share with ya about some past games that I recall watching. Enjoy the fun of the game of football as its seen through my eyes. The eyes of a true Steeler fan as I watch the team that I have admired from childhood, climb the Stairway to Seven.

Here We Go Steelers . . . . Here We Go!!!!

By the way. My Super Bowl picks
Pittsburgh vs. Green Bay.

See ya in Dallas!

FALCONS @ STEELERS
SEPT.12TH,2010

The season begins . . . for Pittsburgh today

With no Big Ben . . . to lead the way

But its ok . . . were calm and cool

Were still gonna play . . . and beat these fools

To count us out . . . that's just absurd

After all . . . there just a bunch a birds

So bring it Falcons . . . give us all your sass

Were the Steelers . . . and were gonna kick your ass

Go Steelers!

What a way to have to start this book. The Falcons? There an NFC team. There just really isn't that much history between the two teams. They have only played each other 13 times and the Steelers won 11 of those games. Falcons won 2 and 1 game ended in a tie. Unfortunately, the game that ended in a tie is the one that stands out in my mind the most. Why was it unfortunate. Well. I'll tell ya why.

It was November 10th, 2002. The Steelers had a 34 to 17 lead going into the 4th quarter. Tommy Maddox was having the best day of his career. He ended up throwing for 473 yards. 4 TD's and 1 pick. It was unreal. Game was in the bag, right?

Introducing Mike Vick. DAMn this guy. He couldn't be stopped. He ran all over us in the fourth quarter and tied up the game. Overtime was a coaches strategy game. Both teams ended up blocking field goals and there was no points scored. James Farrior blocked the field goal for Pittsburgh that left one second on the clock. Maddox threw a hail mary. Holy crap, Burress caught it. BIGGer holy crap. He is a half a yard short of the end zone. Game over! Final score. 34-34.

Well. Enough of this. Lets get on with todays game.

We all know about the Roethlisberger suspension by now. Its all good. He's out for 4 games. My opinion. We win 2 outa these 4 and were good to go. So today we got Dennis Dixon starting at quarterback. No problem. We are a defensive team. Right? Well. It's a good thing for defense cause Dixon was awful shaky. It was a field goal game the whole way. Jeff Reed came in with 39 seconds left in the game to attempt the winning kick. 40 yarder. No problem right? Reed is automatic from here . . . . He freakin missed. You gotta be kiddin me. WTF??? Ok . . . Here we are. Its Atlanta and were heading to over time again. This isn't happening.

Great. Atlanta wins the friggin coin toss. There getting the ball. Like I said. Good thing for defense! Atlanta had to punt. Pittsburgh punted the ball right back to em though, and during the return, Atlanta got a holding call which placed the ball on the 9 yard line. This is good. We got em pinned deep. After a short run and a quick slant pass, they had a first down. CRAP. C'mon D. Before ya know it, there out to the 24 yard line. UhOh . . . wait a minute . . . holding on Atlanta 10 yds. Repeat 3rd down . . . now were talkin. A little incomplete pass to follow and we are in business baby. Atlanta has to punt. Good deal! After the punt we end up with great field position. Were at the 50 yard line. Pittsburgh just wants to run the ball and try to put us into field goal range. Ok no problem! On the first play we hand off to Mendenhall. He runs off right tackle. He bust loose. HE IS

GONE. TOUCH DOwn baby. Final Score. Pittsburgh 15. Atlanta 9. This makes 8 straight opening day victories for the Steelers. Longest current streak in the NFL!

Photo by **Shawn Barton**

Win number one . . . to start our season
An overtime win . . . but still very pleasing
Those dirty birds musta had glue on there beaks
They stuck to us hard . . . like some kinda freaks.
But just like I said . . . when the game came to pass
Hey Falcons . . . We kicked your DAMN ASS!!
Go Steelers

3rd longest overtime touchdown run in NFL history. I think
we found something we were missing in this kid. Good job
Rashard!

STEELERS @ TITANS
SEPT.19TH,2010

We head down to Nashville . . . to take on the Blue

The Tennessee Titans . . . in week number two

A win here today . . . is important you know

I gives us chance . . . to start two and O

So now is the time . . . we need James and Troy

To take off the gloves . . . and BITCH SLAP these boys

Go Steelers!

What comes to my mind when I think Titans and Steelers? Bum Phillips and the Houston Oilers. That's what! After all. Where did the Titans come from? Man those were some games back in the Late 70's. The two AFC Championship games in 78 and 79 were memorable to say the least.

During the 1978 season, the Steelers went 14-2 but one of those losses came to the Houston Oilers. The Oilers had this Huge rookie running back by the name of Earl Campbell and I do mean he was huge! This guys legs were bigger than a normal mans waist. He was running all over the NFL and earned 1978 Rookie of the Year honers, then he met up with a defense like no other. The "Steel Curtain"

During the regular season Monday night win over Pittsburgh, Campbell managed to run for 89 yards and score 3 touchdowns against the Steelers but the AFC Championship game was a whole different story. Carying the ball 22 times in this game he was held to just 62 yards and fumbled the ball 3 times. He just couldn't outrun the gang tackling of the Best defensive unit ever in the game. The Steelers just totally dominated this game winning 35 to 5.

The following season brought a rematch of this game. Again it was the Steelers and the Oilers in the AFC Championship! This game is now known as "The Mike Renfro Game" The Houston fans cried for years over a Renfro catch in the end zone that was ruled outa bounds by the refs. What they seam to forget is even if it was ruled a catch, the Steelers still would have had the lead and Pittsburgh went on to score 10 more points in that game while Houston scored none. Wine all you want Oiler fans. You got beat. Simple as that. As for Campbell. He was held to 15 yds on 17 carries. He never could run against the Steel Curtain defense. But then again, who could?

Pittsburgh won this game 27-13 and with the Oiler loss came one of the most famous quotes in football. At a fan appreciation celebration, The Oilers coach, Bum Phillips, stood on the podium with tears in his eyes and made this famous statement regarding the 2 consecutive losses to Pittsburgh in the championship games. I can still hear him saying this!

"Last year we knocked on the door. This year we beat on it. Next year we're going to kick the son of a bitch in."

This statement would prove to be false. The Oilers never returned to another AFC title game. Ok . . . on with today's game.

Was a great win today. The defense forced 7 turnovers and pretty much dominated the game. I don't know guys. Remember what I said about winning 2 out a 4 without Ben? Well. Were 2 and 0 to start the season. I think this is gonna be a good year? Bad news is we lost Dixon and were running out of QB's. The way our defense is playing I think were gonna be just fine. A little interesting fact about this game. The final score was 19 to 11 and is the 3rd game in NFL history to end by that score.

Troy Polamalu

Photo by Shawn Barton

The Defense was awesome . . . on this given day
With a flying Polamalu . . . leading the way
A 2 and 0 start . . . for two thousand ten
That's pretty impressive . . . since we don't have Big Ben
Those Tennessee Titans . . . weren't even a match
That tough Steeler defense . . . simple kicked there ass!
Go Steelers!

STEELERS @ BUCCANEERS
SEPT.26TH.2010

Week number three . . . we play Tampa Bay

A 3 and 0 start . . . would be nice to say

With quarterback woe's . . . Batch gets the call

But our defense is simply . . . the best of em all

So come on James, Troy and LaMarr

Lets show these punks . . . just who we are

Go Steelers!

With the Buccaneers being an NFC team, there isn't really a lot of past history between them and the Steelers. To this date they have only played each other eight times and Pittsburgh has won seven of those eight. I can honestly say that there isn't really any games between them that stand out to me so im just gonna give a recap of todays game. Hope you enjoy?

Well. Charlie Batch, who started the season as a 4th stringer, gets the start at QB today. Dixon is gone for the year. The way are defense is playing, it should be ok. I mean really. The only thing Batch has to do is not turn the ball over and we should be able to win this game. We have already won the two games I said we needed to win to be ok till we get Ben back so this would be a nice bonus win, Right?

First series of the game and Batch throws an interception. Well. So much for no turnovers. Its ok. Let the defense take over. That's just what they did! The Bucs just couldn't really move the ball much which gave Batch plenty of opportunities to redeem himself, Batch gave a pretty good show after the pic. Hell. He threw for 186 yards and 3 touchdowns. Nice, right? He did throw another pic but the game was already iced so we will let that one slide. Batch even had a 24 yard run on 3rd and 6 that set up a Mendenhall TD. Great game Batch. You get my vote for MVP. Mendenhall also had a pretty good game rushing for 143 yards and a touchdown and I will never forget Brett "The Deisel" Keisel rumbling down the field for 74 yards after a tipped ball interception and scoring a touch down. That big bearded wonder can move!!

Final score
Pittsburgh 38, Tampa Bay 13.
We are 3 and 0! Oh Hell Yea!

Photo by Shawn Barton

The Tampa Bay Bucs . . . were no match for us
As for Charlie Batch . . . He gets an A plus
The defense was awesome . . . As always it seams
Im beginning to smell . . . Seven SuperBowl Rings!
Go Steelers!

RAVENS @ STEELERS
ROUND 1
Oct.3rd.2010

The Steelers and Ravens . . . The first time around

Remember one thing . . . You come to our town

We've played without Ben . . . but the defensive has thrived

A 3 and 0 start . . . keeps are hopes alive

So come bring it on . . . you Baltimore Birds

We're ready to fight . . . I give you my word

Go Steelers!

The Baltimore Ravens and the Pittsburgh Steelers. What a rivalry these two teams have become huh? Known as the two most physical teams in the NFL, this is definitely the biggest, modern day rivalry in the game. I mean plain and simply, these teams hate each other and so do most of the fans. Being from Maryland, I have several friends that are Ravens fans and most of them will tell you that I do try to show a little respect. However I do like to have my fun and rub it in a little when the Steelers win. After all, that's what being a football fan is all about, right? One thing I have noticed about Ravens fans though, They don't like to hear much about there roots. They like to think the Ravens team just came about in 1996. Well, that's not exactly true. Your Ravens were not an expansion team, but the rules were changed a little to accommodate you so I guess I can do the same and let your past be your past. Fair enough?

As far as history between these two teams? Although it isn't that old, it is rich to say the least. These guys have played some epic battles. Some of the most physically tough games I've ever saw. I cant really pick one game that's stands out because they were all great games. I'm shore today wont be any different.

This was a tough fought game from both teams as we new it would be. Batch, who began the season as a 4th string QB got the start again. Offense wasn't much of a factor today as both teams were held to under 100 yds rushing. Both defenses played pretty sound football which is pretty well the norm for these two teams. One thing to remember though Baltimore. Ben will be back next time around and things might not be the same. After all, he is your Daddy!!

Baltimore won this game by a score of 17 to 14. They pulled it out in the last few seconds of the game. One major concern I have for the Steelers is the fact that Jeff Reed missed two more field goals today that would have given us the win. That makes 4 misses in 4 games. He only had 4 misses all last season. I hope they can get this figured out. It wouldn't be good going down the stretch and into the playoffs with an unreliable kicker! Congrats Ravens. Enjoy your win. We have another date down the road!

Congrats to the Ravens . . . You won here today

But listen to me . . . as this I must say

A 4th string QB . . . does this make you proud?

And two missed Field Goals . . . That hushed our crowd

So enjoy your win . . . till we meet again

As things will be Different . . . We'll have Big Ben!

Go Steelers!

BYE WEEK
OCT.10TH,2010

The 5th week of the season gives us a bye week which couldn't have come at a better time when you think about it. Ben's suspension is over and he now gets two full weeks to practice with the team to help prepare him for his first start against another division rival next week. The Cleveland Browns.

Lets talk a little about Ben and what he brings to the offense. At 6ft 5in and around 240, this guy gets compared to full backs and linebackers. Any opposing defense will tell ya, he is tough to bring down. Sometimes he simply amazes me. You think they got him sacked and he just pops free and makes play's. Lets see Brady or Manning do this. First sign of a hit there balling up in a ball, falling to the ground and whining and bitchin to the o-line for letting them get hit.
Come on boys. Play a little "Big Boy" football.

Say what you want about Ben. He is one of the all time great quarterbacks. His stats speak for themselves. As a starter, Ben ranks 8th all time in NFL passer rating at 92.5. He is 5th in yards per attempt with an 8.04 average. He has the fourth highest career winning percentage at .704 and is the youngest quarterback to ever win the Super Bowl. Now umm, you so called "experts", if that don't impress ya, lets try a little playoff stats. With a record of 9 wins and 2 losses, Those other two so called great quarterbacks don't quite compare. That's an impressive .818 winning percentage. Brady isn't bad at .737, but Manning don't even belong. His pathetic .473 playoff win percentage shure gives me a reason to call him the best ever?? Yea right?? Simply because Bens style isn't quit as flashy as Brady and Manning he gets left out of the "Great Ones" category but ill tell ya this. When the game is on the line and you need a big play, Ben is the man I want out there. After all, great ones know how to win, right?

CLEVELAND @ PITTSBURGH
OCT.17,2010

Game 1

Its Ben's first game back . . . and guess who's in town
Another division rival . . . those ole pesky Browns
As a conference winner . . . there not really a threat
But a thorn in our side . . . as always you can bet
So come on Big Ben . . . Its time to throw down
Show em who you are . . . and crush these silly clowns!
Go Steelers!

Pittsburgh and Cleveland. Wow does this take me back. Remember Brian Sipe and the Cardiac Kids? Man the games they had in the 70's. They were comparable to the Ravens games of today.

People called it the Turnpike Rivalry. It was something to see. Pure hatred between players. The Steelers were the dominate team and Cleveland knew it but wouldn't admit it! The sad part was, Cleveland was actually pretty good at this time. They just couldn't beat Pittsburgh. They played 20 games during the 70's and Pittsburgh won 15 of those games. Some say Cleveland was good enough to win a Super bowl at that time. Guess we will never know?

Disappointingly, The Steelers and Browns never met in the playoffs during the 70's. It just never worked out to that. As good as the Browns were, they only made one playoff appearance during that error. That happened in 1971 and they lost to the Colts in the first round. At that time, The AFC Central Division was considered the toughest division in football and was made up of the Steelers, Oilers, Bengals, and Browns. Is it any wonder the didn't get to the post season much?

The game.

Today is the Big Day! Big Ben Day. He is back! As he entered the field the crowd cheered loudly. This had to make him feel more comfortable considering everything that has happened. I myself was very pleased that the fans stood behind him. After all, He is our Super Bowl winning quarterback. What a day he had. He threw for 257 Yds and 3 touchdowns. Not bad for your season opener huh?

The Pittsburgh defense was tough once again. James Harrison was all over the field and made some huge impact plays. This guy is something to watch. He can just plain hit!

Pittsburgh won this game pretty soundly. The final was 28 to 10. Were now 4 and 1 and looking real good for that playoff run. Those damn Ravens are stayin right with us though. Oh well. Wouldn't be the same if they didn't!

As he came on the field . . . The crowd they did cheer
Ben made it back . . . his first game of the year
He didn't let us down . . . as he put on a show
Didn't surprise me . . . He's a winner you know
He had a great game . . . and threw three touchdowns
Was more than enough . . . to bury the Browns

Go Steelers!
Welcome Back Big Ben!

An interesting note. Ben is now 10
and 1 against the Browns

Photo by **Shawn Barton**

STEELERS @ DOLPHINS
OCT.24TH,2010

We head to Miami . . . to catch us some fish

With playoff dreams . . . and a Super Bowl wish

The Dolphins think . . . they'll rule the sea

But a dam of Steel . . . is what we'll be

The Steeler wrath . . . it shall be felt

When this ones over . . . your Tuna Melt

Go Steelers!

Back in the early 70's, the Miami Dolphins were . . . well . . . they were pretty damn good. With names like Griese and Zonka, there offense was pretty potent, but It was the defense that surprised everyone. They really had no big name players but were dominating games. The were known as "The No Name Defense" For three straight years they were in the Super Bowl. In 1971 they lost to the Dallas Cowboys, but the next two would belong to them beating the Redskins in 72 and The Vikings in 73. The 1972 season was incredible. They went a perfect 17 and 0. They remain the only team to have a "perfect season." Teams didn't play quit as many games back in those days but its still an amazing season no matter how you look at it. I Guess you could say these guys were the big dogs on the block, but, little did they know, Rover was about to get boned!

While all this was going on, the Steelers were working there way up the ladder. They were getting great draft picks from Chuck Knoll. There defense was getting stronger every year and The Steel Curtain came to life. Guess what Rover. A bigger, better breed of dog was in charge now. Your rein is over! The Steelers took over as the dominate team in 1974 and it hasn't changed much since. At least you (Miami) got to win a few games before all this huh? Your not going to win today though.

Wow. What a game huh? Miami didn't roll over like I figured they would. They played us tough. Went right down to the wire. This end zone fumble? I'm not to shore. I've watched the video over and over. Ben had his arm around it but??? Oh well. We got the win and we will take it! The refs did the right thing. No evidence, No turn over. I agree with the call. I'd tell ya if I didn't. One thing I saw though was our Defense wasn't quite as aggressive. Maybe that fine from last week on Harrison took a little away from us. Fining a football player for playing football. What a scheme huh? One of Goodells better ideas. I love this guy Goodell! What a . . . naa . . . I wont say it.

Well. We got the win. It wasn't pretty and people will say we shouldn't have won, but a win is a win. I gotta give it to Big Ben though. He showed guts with that dive into the end zone. He has proven to me many times that he is team player and a winner and this is just one more of those times. Most QB's wouldn't even consider a stunt like that. They'd be afraid there ego's would get hurt . . . or maybe there wallets . . . Great job Ben!!!

Final score
Steelers 23. Dolphins 22

It wasn't pretty . . . but still its done
Road wins are tough . . . so we'll take this one
Controversy . . . was the issue
now the Dolphins . . . need a tissue
You can cry all you like . . . but we still won
Need a towel? . . . I got a Yellow one
Go Steelers!

An interesting stat from today's game.

Hines Ward has now caught passes in 184 straight games and has passed **Art Monk** for the 4th longest streak in NFL history. A catch in next weeks game will put him in 3rd place ahead of **Terrell Owens**. You are the man **Hines!**

PITTSBURGH @ NEW ORLEANS
OCT.31,2010

The New Orleans Saints . . . The winners last season
So enjoy if fans . . . you do have reason
But lets not forget . . . you were a disgrace
Your fans wore bags . . . to cover there face
So chant your "Who Dat" . . . and try to act mean
Cause we are the Steelers . . . a real football team
So im gonna tell ya . . . a simple little fact
Your still the "AINTS" . . . how you like that?
Go Steelers!

Ya know. Throughout the season so far, as I was posting my Steelers poems and quotes, I have encountered fans of all the opposing teams. Most of which were not offended in the least of my jokingly insultive rhymes of there team and many even complimented me on them and said they enjoyed my writings. Not you Saints Fans. What a bunch of obnoxious fools. I've received everything from hate mail to threats of violence from you idiots. Now I am sure that there are some class Saints fans out there, but at this time it sure doesn't seam like it. I mean gimme a break here Saints. For years you were considered the scum of the NFL. Your fans even wore bags over there faces to hide there shame of your team. You finally get a decent team and won one, yes one, Super Bowl and all of a sudden you Saints fans think you're the gift to the world and you act as if your team is the best team in the history of football. Sorry about your luck chumpies. You got a long way to go till you can say that.

Let me clue you in on a little secrete about being the greatest team in history. Consistency is where its at. Winning one Super Bowl means one thing. Your Team had one good season. It is a great accomplishment for any team to win the Super Bowl but it has been done by numerous teams so it is not a spectacular feat. Now win two your doing something.

Win 4 . . . Now that's spectacular. Win six . . . Now you are the greatest team in history.

When you have achieved a goal that is unmatched by any other team, when you set the standard for all other teams, when you are the team that all other teams wanna be . . . then you are the greatest team in history. Only one team fits this description.

The Pittsburgh Steelers!

So enjoy your 2009 Super Bowl win Saints fans. You deserve it, but don't ever compare yourselves to the Steelers cause you are not even in the same category and it is doubtfull you ever will be. You'll be back to the bags over your heads in no time at all. As for the insults and threats, you simply show you class as football fans. Maybe the team should wear bags over there helmets and be ashamed of you!

Now. On to the Game.

Im really not sure what happened here today. The Steeler offense just didn't seam to click. Ben still doesn't seam as if he is completely settled in. Hopefully he will get on track next week. He is the man we need to perform. We know he is capable. He'll come around.

As for the Defense, well, they looked great in the first half. The knocked Brees around at will it seamed like. The second half looked like a different team out there. They just couldn't get to Brees at all. I guess they are the defending champs. Lets just put this one behind us and move on. Shall we?

Final Score
Steelers 10 . . . Saints 20

Your still the Aints
Go Steelers!

PITTSBURGH @ CINCINNATI
NOV.8TH,2010

Cincy Always . . . plays us tight
But Pittsburgh shines . . . on Monday night
Division rivals . . . as we know
Its shure to be an awesome show
Bengal tigers . . . whats all that?
More like . . . little pussy cats
So come on Steelers
Play hard and fast
And kick a little kitty ass!
Go Steelers!

The Steelers and the Bengals. Would you call these two teams a rivalry? Well. They have been in the same division since the AFL NFL merger in 1970 and have played each other twice in a season every year since then (except the 1982 strike season) so yes, I think they qualify as a rivalry. The Steelers have pretty much dominated the win loss record winning 50 of 82 games but the Bengals have always seamed to be a thorn in our side. Even during the "Bungal" years in the 1990's they always seamed to play us tough. In 1999. The Bengals finished 4 and 12 but 2 of there wins were against the Steelers. Just goes to show, Division games are different. The teams know each other and it makes for some very exciting games. Back in the 70's these two teams had some remarkable games against each other, but the most memorable game to me has to be the 2005 playoff game. This is the only time these teams have met in the post season, and it was a good one.

This game took place on Jan. 8, 2006 following the 05 season. The Bengals had won the division and the Steelers made the playoffs on a wild card. The Steelers were a 5 point underdog going into the game and no one really gave them a chance. Well. The doubters again. Go figure! The Steelers defense took out QB, Carson Palmer on the second play of the game. Despite this, The Bengals managed to gain a 10 point lead under back up QB, Jon Kitna.

But that would be about all for the Bungals. The Steelers would score 24 unanswered points with some big plays from Big Ben and the Defense forced 3 turnovers to help seal the game in a 31 to 17 Steeler victory. The Steelers went on to win out in the playoffs and would ultimately win our 5th Super Bowl ring as a result of this victory. Once again . . . We prove to all haters . . .

We are the team . . . all other teams . . . wanna be!!
Go Steelers!

Ok. Lets get to tonight's game. It's a Monday night game and we all know what that means. The Steelers rarely loose on Monday night . . . Right? . . . Specially since Ben came to town. It is all looking pretty good tonight again. The Steelers took a 17 to 7 lead into the 4th quarter and extended it to a 27 to 7 lead early in the 4th. Not so fast though. The Bengals mounted a comeback and tried to make this a game. They scored 14 unanswered points to make it 27 to 21 and get within tying range. Jeff Reed had the chance to make it a 2 score game but missed yet another field goal. What is going on with this guy. I think his foot fell off. We have got to have a reliable kicker. He has got me baffled??? Anyhow. Pittsburgh held on for the win after an interception by Polomalu and we are now sitting at 6 and 2. Not bad for a team who was supposed to loose there first 4 games, huh??

Final Score 27 to 21

Half Way through!

Were at the half way point in the season and were sittin on a 6 and 2 record. I'm impressed. The AFC is ours for the taking if we play our cards right. We have the Patriots, Jets and Ravens all with the same record, but at this point, I'd say we are in the drivers seat. Are biggest challenge is the Ravens. They have us beat on the tie breaker ruling so we need to get a step up on em. Lots of season left so well see what happens.

One thing I would like to say a little about is the Roger Goodell issue and fining our players, namely James Harrison, for bad hits. Hey Roger. There football players and all there lives they are trained to hit hard and play the game to the best of there ability. Let them play like they know how and stop trying to take the toughness out of the game. Its what its about and what we as fans want to see. Too bad you cant get fined for stupidity! You would be broke. They know the risk's when they get into the game! A word of advice Roger. The game of football belongs to us. The Fans. Not you. You don't belong here Roger. Your ruining our game!

James Harrison

Photo by Shawn Barton

NEW ENGLAND @ PITTSBURGH
NOV. 14TH, 2010

The Patriots dressed . . . in Red White and Blue
What? . . . They think there America's team too?
We all know . . . as Steeler fans
No one represents . . . like we can
Six Super Bowl titles . . . is what we boast
And Black and Gold . . . flies coast to coast
So come on Pittsburgh . . . couldn't be sweeter
On Sunday night . . . STOMP Those cheaters
Go Steelers!

Since 2000, The Patriots have been called the Dynasty of the decade. They lay claim to three Super Bowl titles and an 18 and 1 season that ended in a Super Bowl loss to the Giants during this span and have made the playoffs 7 out of 10 times in the last ten years. All pretty impressive I certainly have to say! And that Brady, love him or hate him he has shore proven that he can win. Problem is, he keeps beating us!

Coming in to tonights game, Brady is boasting a 5 and 1 record against the Steelers. He just seams to have a knack for picking our defense apart. I give the man credit, he isn't as dumb as he looks. Even through the Belichick cheating scandal he has certainly kept his cool against us. His one loss to the Steelers was a rather significate one though. During the 2004 season the Cheatriots Came into Pittsburgh with a 21 game unbeaten streak and watched it end at the hands of the Steelers defense. You cant win em all Brady!

Something a gotta say about this Belichick scandal. Come on Bill. I mean really. Cheating?? You are supposed to be a head coach. You have accomplished one thing from all of this though. You have tainted your teams image for life. Congrats Coach. Great job!!

For Tonights game, Well Brady, you did it again. You stayed on top of the defense all night and pulled off another win over the mighty Pittsburgh Steelers. What more can I say. You seam to have our number. Remember Brady, All good things end eventually. Hope to see you in the playoffs Cheatriots!

Final score
Pittsburgh 26
New England 39

ok . . . on that note . . . .
have a great night . . .
have a great dream . . . .
my money is still . . . .
on that Pittsburgh team!!!
Go Steelers!

Interesting facts of the game.

Hines Ward's streak of 186 consecutive games with a reception was ended in this game as he was taken out with a concussion.

Jeff Reed missed another chip shot field goal. Come on Jeff. Get with it man!

OAKLAND @ PITTSBURGH
NOV.21ST,2010

Black and Silver . . . Black and Gold
Brings back memories . . . days of old
The immaculate reception was just the beginning
of a team full of character, pride, and winning
Bradshaw, Franco, Lambert n Swann
Live in my mind like a favorite song
A few years later the names have changed
But Steeler Pride always remains
So come on Pittsburgh . . . keep tradition rockin
with a good ole fashioned
Raider ASS STOMPIN
Go Steelers!

The Steelers and Raiders huh? Now this is some football history. Back in the early 70's, this is what it was all about. The Raiders were known as the bad asses on the block and also the dirtiest players in the game. Mind you, they made a rep on that. With John Madden at the helm who could expect anything else? His motto was "knock there friggin heads off" Well. In 1972, The Raiders got there heads knocked off by a play called the "Immaculate Reception"

The most famous play in football history!

I will never forget it. Bradshaw threw the ball hard on a rope to John "Frenchy" Fuqua. Jack Tatum, known as the dirtiest player in the game and righteously so, hit Frenchy just as the ball got to him and the ball was deflected in the air. Franco Grabbed it by a shoelace catch and took it into the end zone for a touchdown. The play has been controversial ever since but started the dynasty we all know as the 6 time Super Bowl Champ **Pittsburgh Steelers.**

Lets discuss this play a little. Shall we? At this time. The ruling in football was "If a ball was deflected off an offensive player and another offensive player recovered it, it could not be advanced" Now, John Madden argues to this day that it was an illegal play. Forget about it John. It was legal cause your man Jack Tatum, who you taught to be dirty, tipped the ball in the air making it a totally legal play. Results. You loose. We win. Get over it John!

The start of a Dynasty begins!
This play would prove to be fate as the Steelers would go on to dominate the AFC. The Raiders and there fans still cry about it. Lets see. Will they be crying today?

What a game. Despite the refs efforts to try and take the Steelers completely out of the game, it was a massacre. The Steelers were penalized 14 times for a team record 163 yards but still managed to win the game in "Steel Curtain" fashion. A little message to Roger Goodell. Hey Roger. We all know you hate the Steelers and do not want them to win but really Rog. Instructing the refs to penalize our players for anything they can? You show real class. Get out of our game. You don't belong here!

Final score

Pittsburgh 35
Oakland 3

Hey Richard Seymour. I'll bet you punch your wife when she isn't looking too. Lmao. What a joke. You deserve to be suspended!

The striped shirts tried to ruin our day
so UP yours refs . . . we played anyway
The Raiders did some talkin and trashin
so we kicked there ass . . . in STEELER fashion
Go Pittsburgh

Number 32. "**Franco Harris**" The man who started it all!

Photo by Shawn Barton

PITTSBURGH @ BUFFALO
NOV.28TH,2010

Buffalo is going for three straight wins . . .

but Blitzburg's in town . . . so that streak could end . . .

James and Troy will lead the way . . .

Do ya think we might pay some fines today?

So come on Pittsburgh . . . keep your cool . . .

Cause these Buffalo Bills . . . There a bunch of bull . . . Shit!

Go Steelers!

The Steelers and Bills have kind of an interesting comparison. They have both dominated the AFC at one time or another. I mean you can't deny the Bills. They are the only team in history to go to 4 straight Super Bowls. They may have lost all four, but they still got there. That is an incredible accomplishment. During the early 90's the Bills were tough to beat. With players like Jim Kelly and Thurman Thomas who could expect anything less, but the game that I recall as one of the best games between the Steelers and the Bills was the 1996 playoff game. Let me tell you why.

Coming into this game the Bills had won there last ten AFC post season games and had been in four of the last five Super Bowls. They also seamed to have Pittsburgh's number and had beat them seven of there last ten meetings. That would all change abruptly. The Steelers wooped up on the Bills in this game and basically ended there streak as an AFC dominate team. The final score was 40 to 21 and the Steelers went on to the Super Bowl. Unfortunately they lost to the Cowboys. Many people say that this game was paid off as Neil Odonell, who was usually a very accurate passer, through two ridiculous interceptions. I don't think he was paid off. I think he just frikking choked !

He was never that good anyways . . .

Now lets check out today's game.

Well. What can I say here? The Steelers took a 13 point lead into the half but just could hold the Bills off and let them tie it up. Once again, penalties were an issue. James got another personal foul penalty and I'm shore a fine will follow. He is already over the $100,000.00 mark in fines for this season. So we head into over time again. it's a good thing we signed a new kicker cause we definitely needed him. We got a big break from a Bills dropped pass and Suisham kicked the winning field goal. His fourth of the day. Wow. That was too close for comfort . . .

Hines Ward continues to add to the Steelers record books by recording his **28**th career 100 yard receiving game today extending his own record. Great Game Hines.

Hines Ward

Photo by Shawn Barton

Buffalo put up . . . a hell of a fight
But we won this battle . . . man that was tight
We went to New York . . . and won one more
I all can say is . . . Next week . . . Look out Baltimore!!!!
Go Steelers

PITTSBURGH @ BALTIMORE
ROUND 2
DEC. 5TH,2010

This ones for my good friend Jess . . .

She Thinks the Ravens are the best . . .

Us Steeler fans . . . We all know . . .

Pittsburgh's always been the show . . .

You lucked out once . . . early this year . . .

but this time around . . . Ben is here . . .

So sorry Jess . . . something i gotta do . . .

Hey DIRTY BIRDS . . . . PLUCK YOU!!! . . . .

Go Steelers!

Here we go again. The Steelers and the Raven's in a fight for the AFC North title. What is it about these two teams that make football so exciting? Could it be the fact that they are very similar in many ways? I mean take a look at these two defenses. Year after year they battle at being the best in the league. Could it be the fact that both of these teams thrive on toughness and intimidation to beat there opponents down? Lets face it. These are the two most physical teams in the NFL. They are just plain scary, but the real reason why these two teams are so exciting to watch, they just hate each other and that makes for some fun football.

As I look back at the history between these two teams and try to find one game that really stands out as the most memorable, I cant! Every game they play is a memorable game. Its impossible to pick just one! Every time these two teams step on the field together, it is going to be a fight to the finish and sometimes a bloody fight. What more can a fan ask to see? Speaking of fans, sometimes there is just as much action in the stands as there is on the field. Steelers fans and Raven fans do not play well together. There is only one thing that could be better than watching a game between these teams and that would be watching the two best, most dominate teams in the NFL, meet in the Super

Bowl. Unfortunately, this will never happen as they are both in the AFC. Too bad. Would be the best Super Bowl ever! What a game today huh? It was a defensive battle just like we all knew it would be, but how about the guy they call

"Big Ben"

You wanna talk toughness. Ben started today's game on a broken foot. Lets see Manning or Brady do that! They wont play with a broken finger nail, but the foot was just the start of it. In Pittsburgh's first offensive series, Ben was inadvertently hit in the face and suffered a broken nose from the deal. Did this stop him? Not a chance, as he went on to pass for 253 yards and a touchdown. His performance today was nothing less than heroic and showed his dedication to his teammates. You are definitely one of the great ones **Big Ben**, as I know of no other player, past or present, that could have done what you did today.

Baltimore had us on the ropes most of the day. They took an early lead and held it into the fourth quarter. It looked like they may have us beat until the "Playmaker" Troy Polamalu created a huge fumble which Lamar Woodley picked up and returned to the 9 yard line setting up are only touchdown. It was a short dump pass to Redman who showed great effort by breaking two tackles on his way to the end zone. Pittsburgh's defense sealed the win by stopping the Ravens on 4th down with 33 seconds left in the game. It wasn't pretty, but I'll take it.

Steelers Win! Final Score. 13 to 10
It was a fight that we just saw . . .
Bitter rivals in a braw . . .
You broke Ben's nose . . .
But in the game he would stay . . .
And Troy came through with an awesome play . . .
Now were in first and thats a fact . . .
We kicked some stinkin RAVEN Ass . . .
Go Steelers . . .

It seams that many of you Ravens fans seam to think that breaking Bens nose makes your team the Bad Asses of the AFC North. Simple put . . . you did not do it on purpose and it was merely an accidental result of a football play. Further more, I believe that Ben continued to play after that and also was playing on a broken foot and beat you. Now. Who is the Bad Ass?

CINCINNATI @ PITTSBURGH
DEC. 12, 2010

Cincy's back For another try . . .
They wanna knock us off our high
There playoff hopes are already done
So there lookin to spoil are Super Bowl run
Those ugly orange tigers
could be dangerous today
They have nothing to loose
There just here to play
We need this win
A loss could be bitter
So bury those wussies
in kitty litter

Go Steelers!

With this being the second meeting of the season between the Bengals and the Steelers, I'm going to go straight to the game recap on this one as I've already covered my memories in the fist meeting.

With a final score of 23 to 7 you would think that this game was kind of a blowout, but no such luck. Cincy actually played us pretty tight as they always do. Our two touchdowns came from the defense as Ben and the offense just couldn't get the ball in the end zone. We dominated the time of possession but the only offensive scoring came by way of 3 field goals.
Thank god we got a new kicker earlier this year huh?

Hats off to Polamalu and Woodley who each had a pick six in this game giving us our only two touchdowns. Troy had two picks in the game. Carson Palmer, who by the way was Troy's room mate at USC, told reporters that Polamalu is the best defensive player in the NFL right now. I have to say I would agree. Troy did re-injure his ankle in this game but stayed in, so hopefully its nothing serious.

Once again it wasn't pretty, but a win is a win. Were sitting at 10 and 3 and after 13 games, our defense has still not given up a 100 yard rusher this season. Pretty impressive in my book. Oh Yea. We are still in first place as well !

The defense played . . . for all its worth

And helped us clinch . . . a playoff berth

Troy's the man . . . with two nice picks

He knows all . . . of Carsons tricks

Good job Pittsburgh . . . you kept your cool

And took those little kitties . . . to school

Go Steelers

Welcome to the playoffs Steeler Fans!

Slightly overshadowed by Troys big day, Steelers WR Hines Ward had eight catches for 115 yards against the Bengals, giving him 944 career receptions. That puts him 10th all time, surpassing Art Monk. Great job Hines!!

NEW YORK JETS @ PITTSBURGH
DEC. 19TH. 2010

The Steelers and Jets . . . do battle today
We dont have Troy . . . or Miller by the way
A win in this game . . . and a loss from the Raven's
Will give us the North . . . We'll win the division
So "Here we go Steelers" . . . dont let this one pass
tear off there wings . . . and ground some Jet ass!
Go Steelers

You know, there is something I find interesting about the history between the Steelers and the Jets. Simply, they don't have much of a history. Prior to today's game they have only met 19 times. That is a very low number considering they are both AFC teams. I cant really recall any games that stand out in my mind between these teams. The positive I see is that Pittsburgh has won 16 of the 19 meetings. That's not that surprising though as the Jets really have not been historically a dominate team.

One thing I will say about the Jets is that under coach Rex Ryan, they have gotten a little better, but I still cant stand listening to Rex make his little speeches. Confidence is one thing but being a big mouthed, arrogant ass is another. A little clue Rex. Until you win a Super Bowl you are not the best team in the NFL. You have had your chances and failed miserably. Get over yourself. Your not that good.

On to today's game.

Its ok Rex. I'm just funnin !

What can I say. The Jets jumped on us early by retuning the opening kickoff for a touchdown and never looked back. The Steelers tried to make a game of it but without Troy out there on defense we just couldn't hold them down. Hopefully he'll be back next week. You may have won today Rex, but keep something in mind. This is only the 4th win in Jets history over the Steelers and I certainly hope we meet you in the playoffs with a healthy Polamalu. Go give one of your famous after game speeches Rex and boast about your team and how great they are. When you get a ring, let me know. I doubt it will ever happen though.

Final score

Jets 22 Steelers 17

Ok so we lost . . . its all good . . .

we still made the playoffs . . . like we knew we would . . .

we get our guys back to make that big run . . .

for ring number seven . . .

cause were the Steelers . . . WE ARE number ONE . . . .

Go Steelers . . .

CAROLINA @ PITTSBURGH
DEC.23RD 2010

The Steelers and Panthers . . . A Thursday night game . . .

They have nothing to loose . . . There records pretty lame . . .

Wearing powder puff blue . . . how tough can they be? . . .

Look more like panzies . . . than Panthers to me . . .

To keep our 2 seed . . . we need to play Phat . . .

So come on Pittsburgh . . . Lets skin us some Cats . . .

Go Steelers . . .

With the Carolina Panthers being an expansion team as well as an NFC team, there's just not any history to go on here, so I'm just going to skip right to the game.

We need to win this one to claim are 2 seed in the playoffs and get at least one home field game. The Panthers come in to this game with only 2 wins, so despite some injuries, we should come away with a win here.

Well. Like I said the Panthers only have 2 wins and it showed. Big Ben set a new career high today by throwing for 259 first half yards. He also threw for 1 touchdown and ran for another to help secure the win. Just one more regular season game to go. Bring on the Cleveland Clowns !

Final score

Pittsburgh 27 Carolina 3

Another win and it was sweet . . .
Those Panthers just couldn't take the heat . . .
This one was simple . . . nuthin fancy . . . .
I told ya they were a bunch of panzies . . .
Go Steelers . . .

HAPPY NEW YEARS STEELER FANS !

PITTSBURGH @ CLEVELAND
JAN. 2ND 20111

We head in to Cleveland . . .

to take on the Browns . . .

There gonna be trying . . .

to take us down . . .

Its really quite simple . . .

are goal is clear . . .

Win this game . . .

we win the division this year . . .

Troy should be in . . .

I hope so anyway . . .

He's always the man . . .

to make a big play . . .

These guys can be pesky . . .

this is a fact . . .

So lets go Pittsburgh . . .

Time to kick some Clown ASS . . .

Go Steelers . . .

Another division Game today against the Browns and the final game of the 2010 regular season. A win today secures a first round bye and the 2010 AFC North division title. How sweet that would be but remember, we are playing the Browns so it is not a given win. Even though the Browns have a loosing record, they are a division rivalry and anything can happen in division games. I covered most of the history between these two teams in the first meeting so lets just get to today's game. There is a lot at stake in this one!

Well. What can I really say here. It was a blowout. Ben didn't even play in most of the second half as the Steelers laughed at the clowns all the way to the end. The regular season is over. Playoffs. HERE WE COME !

Congratulations to the 2010 AFC North division champs !

Final score

Pittsburgh 41 Cleveland 9

I believe the final . . . was Fourty One to Nine . . .

I told ya before hand . . . it was ass whoopin time . . .

What a great game . . . we all got to see . . .

We are Division Champs . . . Just like we should be . . .

We are the Steelers . . .

The 2010 AFC North Champs . . .

Troy Polamalu tied a career high in this game with his seventh pick of the season. Way to go Troy !

It's the first round of the playoffs and the Steelers have a bye. The AFC match ups are the Jets against the Colts and the Ravens against the Chiefs. I'm not shore who we will be playing next week but whoever it is, you better be ready cause you will be playing a healthy team in our stadium and that spells trouble for you.

Since the Steelers are off this week I'm going to use this time to mention some standout players from this past season. I am going to call this my "Pride" awards

My "Pride" award for **Best Offensive Player** of the 2010 season goes to **Rashard Mendenhall**. We struggled offensively throughout most of the season and he was simply the work horse that helped us maintain ball control and allowed our defense to dominate games like they did.
He finished the season with 1237 yards and 11 Touchdowns . . .
Congrats Rashard!

My "Pride" award for **Best Defensive Player** of the 2010 season goes to **James Harrison**. Despite all the penalties, all the fines, (and thank you Roonies for backing him) he maintained a level of intensity that not many players have and instilled fear in opponents. He finished the season with 94 tackles,6 forced fumbles, and 2 interceptions . . . Very impressive . . . Congrats James!

My "Pride" award for **Surprise Superstar** goes to Mike Wallace. This guy is gonna be something special. He came up with big plays when we needed him. He finished the season with 1257 yds,10 touchdowns, and an impressive 21 yards per catch average . . . way to go Mike!

Now for the big one. My "Pride" award for **Team MVP** for the 2010 season goes to none other than **Troy Polamalu**. No one else in the NFL had more game changing plays than Troy. He completely changed the outcome of several games that we could have lost. Remember Baltimore? Despite injuries, he still managed to put up 62 tackles,1 forced fumble and 7 interceptions. Congrats Troy. You are the best player I have seen in many years!!

I wanna give an honorable mention to Ben Roethlisberger. Despite all the off season troubles he conducted himself with dignity and Steeler pride! He had a very good year and showed his maturity as a QB . . . One of the best in the game right now! Thanks Ben for a great season!

Well. The first round of the playoffs are over and guess who's coming to town. Non other than the Baltimore Ravens. This is gonna be the game of the year. Maybe better than the Super Bowl itself. Good luck Rat Birds. Your gonna need it !

Its being called everything from World War 3 to Armageddon!!! . . . . Are you ready for this game or what?? . . .

GO STEELERS!!!!

RAVENS @ STEELERS
PLAYOFFS
JAN.15TH 2011

The stage is set . . . The games biggest rival.

The Steelers and Ravens . . . A fight for survival.

An all out war . . . could be a blood bath.

As fans of the game . . . what more could we ask?

So heY STEEler Nation . . . Its time to gET LOud!

Put on your colors . . . and stand up proud.

As for wearin Purple . . . Thats gotta suck.

Bend over birdies . . . your about to get plucked!

Go Steelers.

Birdy, Birdy, on the field . . .
you broke his nose, but now its healed . . .
He's not gonna let this deed just pass . . .
He's comin back to kick yoUR Ass!! . . .
Go Big Ben . . .
Go Steelers . . .

Man what a setting for a playoff game huh? The Ravens and Steelers at Hines Field. Say what you want about New England but the best two teams in the NFL are playing right here today. We split the season with these guys but they have never beat us in a playoff game. Lets hope it doesn't happen today either. Are players have gotten healthy, and Big Ben seams to have the Ravens number so lets get ready to watch the best game we have seen all year.

GO STEELERS !

Wow. What a friggen game! We took an early 7 to 0 lead but Baltimore cam right back and jumped all over us. We went in to half time loosing 21 to 7 and things were looking pretty scary, but thankfully, Pittsburgh scored 14 3rd quarter points and 10 4th quarter points and all the Ravens could manage was 3 more point for the rest of the game. Big Ben played an excellent second half and so did the Steelers defense.

Congrats Pittsburgh on an amazing win. That was definitely the best game of the season and the best game to date between the Ravens and the Steelers.

Next week we will have the winner of the Patriots Jets game. We lost to both these teams this year. Oh well. This is the playoffs. Bring it on!

Despite what the say about New England, the two best teams in The NFL played yesterday in a game that will not be matched. Not even in the Super Bowl . . . That was one of the best played game I have ever watched . . . Steelers fan or Ravens fan . . . what a game!!!!

The dominance of Pittsburgh continues.

Pittsburgh's 31-24 divisional-round victory over the Baltimore Ravens placed the Steelers in the conference title game for an NFL-best 15th time since the 1970 merger. Pittsburgh broke the tie with the Cowboys who has 14 title games and continues to pull away from the San Francisco 49ers who has 12 title games.

Way to go Pittsburgh.
You are the team . . . all other teams want to be !

Defensive Star
Lamarr Woodley

Photo by Shawn Barton

The Steelers will make their 15th conference championship appearance since 1970 (most in the NFL), while improving to 32-19 all-time in the playoffs, including a perfect 3-0 mark against the Ravens. The Steelers' .627 winning percentage is the highest in NFL playoff history as well.

Ok. We got the Jets next week. Bring on Big Mouth!

JETS @ STEELERS
AFC CHAMPIONSHIP
JAN. 23RD 2011

A sea of yellow . . . will wave in the air

The Terrible Towel . . . will fly everywhere

To honer a legend . . . an icon some say

Myron Cope . . . It is his birthday

"YOI" he would say . . . as we beat this team down

"Double YOI" he'll say . . . as we score a touchdown

MAn he'd be proud . . . of the Steelers today

so little green men . . . dont get in our way

You know Pittsburgh . . . it would be his wish

Its Ass kickin time . . . . Lets F*#kin Do This!!!

Go Steelers!!!!

ATTENTION!

Pittsburgh Airport security has been put on full alert following the landing of an aircraft that departed from a New York destination. The craft is believed to be full of desperate, but hardly dangerous, little green men and led by a large fat man with a big mouth. These men are considered to be a nuisance to the city of Pittsburgh and should be hoarded to Heinz Field immediately to await there fate. Thank You!

Well here we are again. The AFC championship game. One win away from the Super Bowl and facing the New York Jets. They beat us in the regular season but if you recall, we were without Troy Polamalu and were pretty banged up in other positions. I've listened to Rex Ryan run his mouth all week and now its time to shut him up and watch him fail again. As one of your players said this past week Rex, "Cant Wait"

Lets rock tough guy!

Pretty good game. Pittsburgh took a 24 to 3 lead in the first half and it was all they would need. The Jets tried to make a comeback in the fourth quarter but it was too little, to late. Once again the Rex Ryan led team fails to accomplish its goal and guess what Steeler Fans. Were in the friggin Super

Bowl. For the 8th time and the 3rd time in the last 6 years, we are the 2010 AFC conference Champions. OH Hell yea !

Pittsburgh Steelers. Super Bowl bound. How familiar does that sound. You know. Its kind of amazing to be a Steeler fan. Looking back through the early 70's and seeing the accomplishments of the Steelers, all I can say is, being a fan of any other team just wouldn't compare. No other team in the NFL can say they have won 6 Super Bowls. No other team in the NFL can say they have been to 8 Super Bowls.

The great players and coaches that have passed through Pittsburgh is simply incredible. Do you realize that since 1969, the Steelers have had only 3 head coaches, and all 3 have won Super Bowls! Pretty wild huh? And Speaking of the players. I am going to take a little time to tell you about my favorite top 10 players of all time. So here they are.

Starting off with #10 is Jack Ham. This guy just played football the way football is supposed to be played. He was tough and knew how to read the QB as well as anyone in the game . . .

At #9 is Mean Joe Greene. He was just plain scary!

#8 is Rocky Bleier. This guy was an unsung hero back in the day . . . . he played on pure heart. For a guy that was injured in a war and told he may never walk again, he shore could run.

#7 on my all time favorite Steelers list is Rod Woodson. Rod played during a time when Dion Sanders was know as the best corner in the NFL. Pure BS! He had nothing on Rod. Dion was a good coverage man but couldn't tackle a ball boy. Rod would hit ya like a freight train and cover with the best of em. Rod finished his career with 71 interceptions.(3rd most), holds the record for career interception return yardage (1,483), and interception returns for touchdowns (12). He was an 11 time Pro Bowler and was inducted into the HOF in 2009. Pretty good career huh?

My #6 all time favorite. Franco Harris. He was just plain fun to watch.

#5 on my all time favorites list is Hines Ward. I don't think I've ever seen another player have as much fun on the football field as he does . . . an he is a tough SOB as well. This guy plays wide receiver and hits like a linebacker . . . You wont see that to often.

My 4th favorite all time Steeler is Jack Lambert. Man was he fun to watch. This guy was just plain mean. By today's standards, he'd pay more fines in a season than he made from his salary. He defined the linebacker position.

My #3 all time favorite Steeler is Troy Polamalu. He plays with a reckless enthusiasm that I've never seen from any other player, past or present.

At number 2 on my all time favorite Steeler list is Lynn Swann. There has never been another receiver in the game who could catch the ball like Swann. His grace, leaping ability and sheer ball concentration allowed him to make catches that would have been impossible for most receivers. This Guy was purely spectacular to watch.

My #1 all time favorite Steeler is gonna shock you all. He never won a Super Bowl. He was never the big star of the game. He just went out and played football and I enjoyed ever moment that he was on the field. His name . . .
Meryl Hoge.

Do you know what day it is? It is Super Sunday! Hell yea. Lets watch the Super Bowl.

SUPER BOWL XLV
PITTSBURGH STEELERS
VS. GREEN BAY PACKERS
FEB. 6TH 2011 @ COWBOYS STADIUM

We are the Mighty Steelers . . . The best there's ever been

So here's to all you doubters . . . that said we couldnt win

They'll never make the playoffs . . . is what the experts told

Sorry bout your luck you fools . . .

were in the SUPER BOWL

So sit back all you haters . . . get comfy if you please

but pay real close attention . . .

were about to shred some cheese

Go Steelers!

A special shout out to the one guy who tried his best but couldn't keep us from making it here.

Hey Roger Goodell !

UP YOURS!

So here we are. In the Super Bowl again. Despite what all the experts said, despite Roger Goodell's constant efforts to keep us from winning, despite QB issues and injuries, we are in the big show once again. Throughout the years, I don't think I've ever been more proud to be a Steelers fan. The odds that this team had to over come to get here were simply incredible. This team played there asses off to get to this game and deserve to be recognized for there efforts. To all you Big Ben doubters, I think he just proved that he is among the elite quarter backs. Don't believe me? Check his stats. Just go back and read the bye week chapter. It speaks for itself.

Ok here we Go. Good luck Pittsburgh. Lets win number 7

Wow. It just wasn't our day huh. If it could go wrong it did. We looked pretty flat out there. Not really shore what to think at this point. I'm to disappointed to think about anything. We got beat and beat soundly. Congrats to Green Bay. What else is there to say?

Was a great season Pittsburgh. Hold your heads high. You did what everyone said you couldn't do.
Steeler fans remember. We are the standard of excellence. We are the team all other teams wanna be!!! Green Bay Packers . . . World Champs . . . I respect that!

See ya next year Steeler Fans

Made in the USA
Middletown, DE
09 September 2024